Rainbow Walking

YEMANA

Rainbow Walking
by Yemana Sanders
Published by Jade Lake Press, East Meredith, New York

ISBN: 978-0692578032

The author may be contacted at yemanazero@gmail.com or on FaceBook.

from me
to you

WHY RAINBOW WALKING?

Our body is a vessel of spirit, walking on earth, a mobile miniature functioning with the same elements of her: earth, fire, water, and air, activated by spirit and ether. When all the elements of the outer earth come together in balance, a perceivable rainbow is created. When our body is awake and in harmonious flow, we are creating a replica of the outer and experience joy and freedom, a rainbow.

Spirit resists programming, the limiting advice of our human tribe which causes us to feel separate and fragmented, blocking the energy flow.

Waking up to what presents itself, becoming conscious, the energy starts to spin, and the inside becomes a mirror image of the rainbow, and starts to shine. Beliefs drop away, and we flow and experience directly all there is.

Mountains and rivers and all the beings residing in the elements are our brothers and sisters, myriad mirrors of our self. Understanding that spirit has an earthly experience in this particular body on mother earth, our spaceship spirals through this universe, exploring . . . seeing simply what is, spirit in action, rainbow body walking!

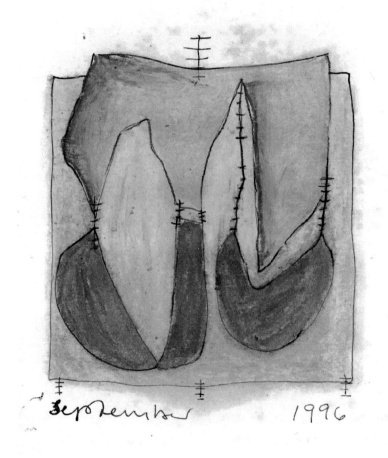

September 1996

Softly my beloved,
open this book of yours.
I will touch you,
multi-leveled
within your heart.
Take a breath,
feel the waves I am sending you.

Receive the gold
to give away.
Express the rainbow,
flood of colors from the beginning of
time.

Receiving-giving,
receiving-giving.
Breathing in,
breathing out.

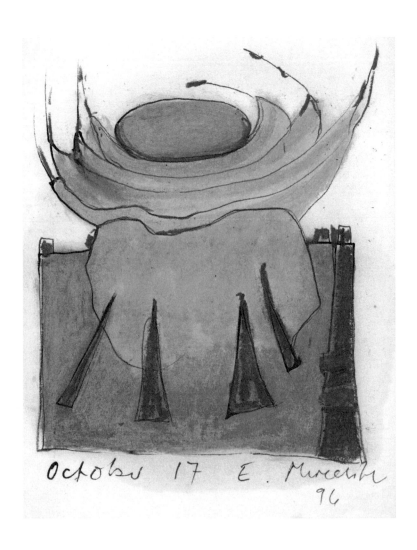

October 17   E. Muccelin
96

4

We are our
own living book,

in form
informing each other,

Softness of heart,
clarity of mind.

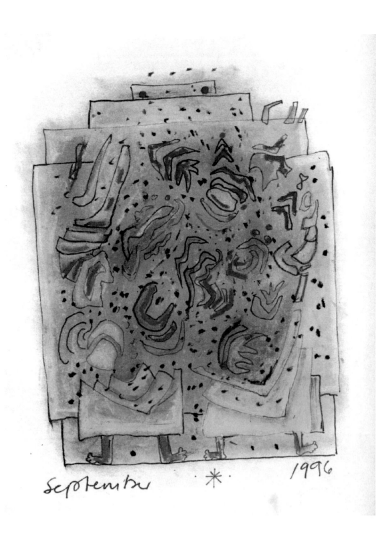

September   ✳.   1996

Rainbow tribe
living on the edge,
where spirit and earth mingle,
masculine and feminine unite
in innocence and
fearlessness.

This is my life's purpose,
celebration
on the altar of love and
understanding.

Crystal beingness of the new dawn,
inviting true communication
intentional listening
nourishing oneness
heartful creation
humble power
radiant spirit
gratefulness.

october 1   1996

In early years
I despised my higher self,
my spirit
asking so much of me,
little self
always limping behind.

Spirit knew so much,
and little self was supposed to live this truth,
manifest its wisdom.

Be
rainbow walking.

October. 18   E Meredith
94

Glittering sound
vibrating vision
millions of little eyes,
soft and hard.

Beloved self. . . here I come,
burning heart
I am returning,
sweet love,
10'000 mirrors in one.

Magnetized into form lattice,
hypnotized into polarization,
veiled in forgetfulness,
looking desperately
for union.

Truth - mirror,
luminous ground,
embracing the spectrum,
illusions of birth
and death.

I am that I am

discriminating wisdom,
demagnetizing,
lifting.

12

Life is a reality
to be experienced,
a mystery,
an opening . . .
not a problem to be solved.

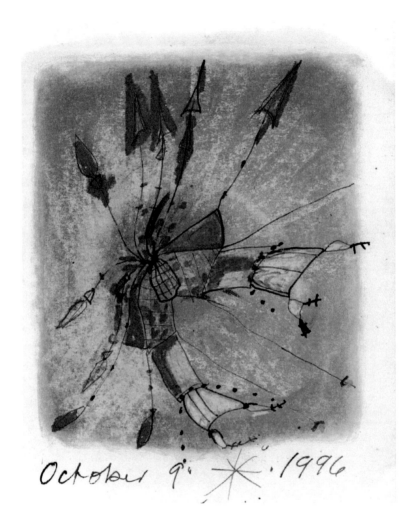

October 9ᵗʰ 1996

I am-
in the beginning,
I am
in the end,
always.

The Karmapa smiles
on his deathbed,

"Where do you think I am going?"

October 17 E Meredith
96

In
conscious,
active image making,
imagination . . .
I see
us within the Great Innate Perfection,

shoulder to shoulder
we walk through
the gate
of
infinite goodness with
no opposites,

true adventure starting now.

October 9   1996

My attitude,
my focus,
creates the world I see.

It is entirely
up to me
how I view
any situation.

November 1996

20

Sovereign diamond,
shine,
let freedom reign.

Head and heart
in
black space of light
are one.

This journey has no distance,
but infinite possibilities
on
luminous ground.

August E. Meredith 1996

Baggage is inefficient thought,
creating more of the same as I go,

discipline is to
"throw it off as quickly as I can."

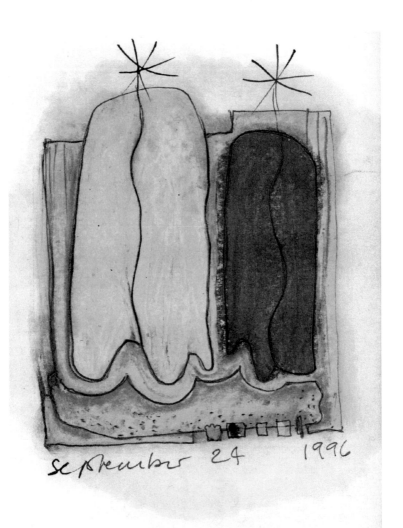

september 24   1996

What I acknowledge
in my neighbor,
I strengthen in
myself.

Listen to the template
of innate perfection,
the mandala of
wisdom and compassion,

mingled in the elements of earth.

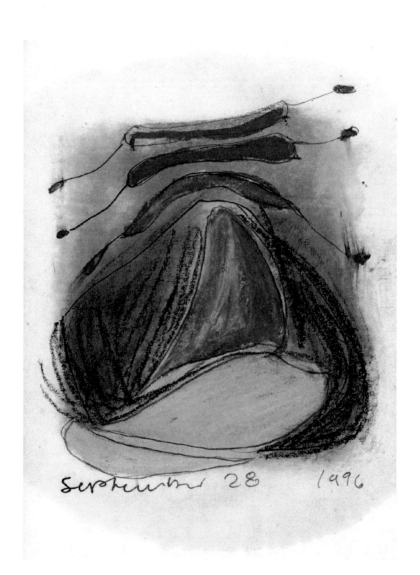

September 28   1996

We're so
involved in surviving,
that dying is
inevitable.

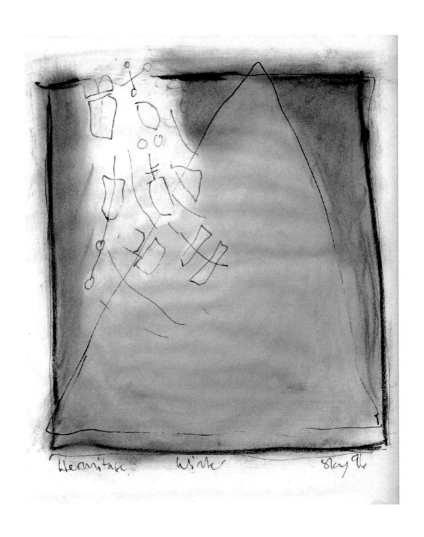

Hermitage   Winter   Skye 96

On the journey,
without distance,

by loving
I am loved,

by giving
I am given,

by understanding
I am understood.

Nowhere to go,
just to be. . .

sailing the rainbow.

October 9 ✳ 1996

How could I ever doubt love,
doubt my innate template,
holy ground?

You
Me
Us

That which has no needs,
just love expanding,

the presence
shining through illusions
of separateness.

When I stop fighting,
nature will bow her head,
the lion and the lamb,
playing.

Distractions
are
endless,

be here,
right now!

November 1996

I am teasing myself
with terrible stories,
near and far. . . .

Can you still see the diamond light?

Through torture and war,
mishap and sickness?

What if something happens to
my kids?

Wrathful deities,
peaceful deities,
in the bardo,

indestructible diamond.

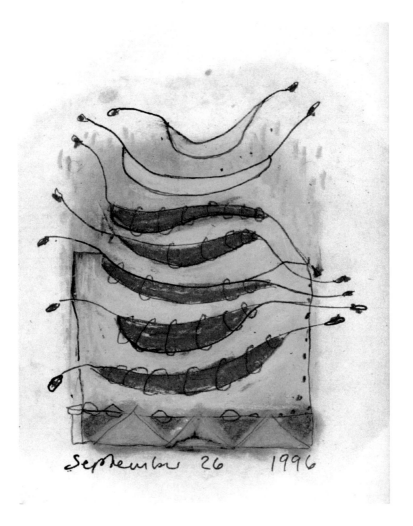

September 26   1996

Be bold,
be sovereign!

I can see her,
the one who resists,
the one who projects,

Caught!

Bringing the old victim back
to source,
freeing her.

September 1976

Being in disguise,
boundaries are shed.

What is welling up
from source
through
aeons of clutter,
is emerging
filament sparkling
without interruption.

Hands
caressing the core.

Octobu 12 E. Meredith
96

Am I trustworthy to myself?

Can I rely on myself
in times of stress,
when my little self has too much to say,
is too reactive,
judgemental,
does not listen enough?

I am to prove to myself
that I can stand here,
rain or shine,
being the servant
of the infinite good.

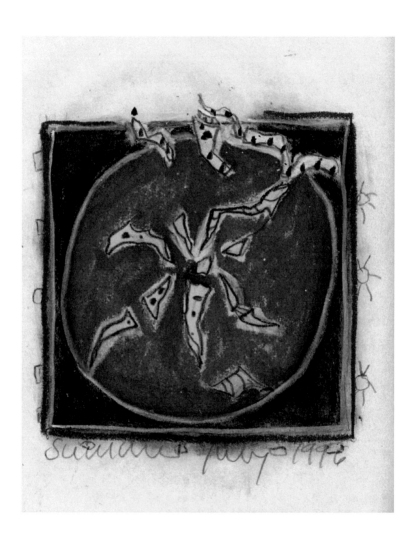

The more I hold,
the less I have. . . .

Why would I ever worry?
I can never loose you!

Even if I exchange this vessel
at the end of this short
life . . .
love prevails.

October 6 1996

44

Bones from space,
assembled in this body,
starclusters signature
sealed on earth.

A cocoon opening.

Taste this apple!

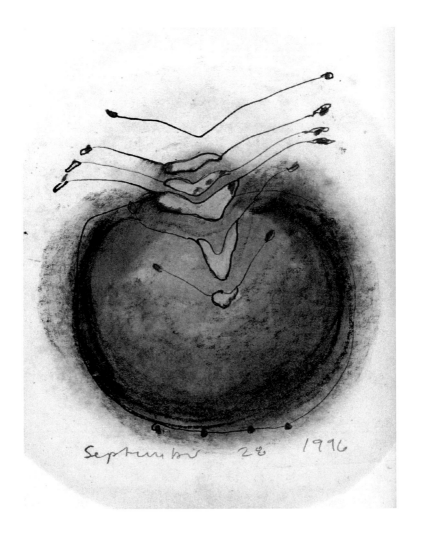

September 2º 1996

I am your muse,
borrowing this vessel,
this library of ancient
knowledge,
stardust memory
of
infinite galaxies,
dancing on earth,
releasing
into freedom's fullness.

August sunny ☼ • 1996

I literally gave
my heart away.
While dying,
I realized,
it had grown
a thousand times!

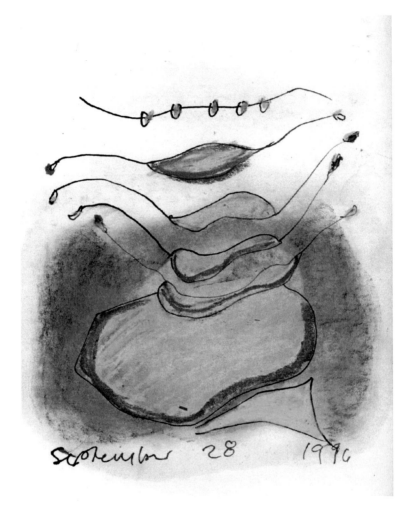

September 28   1996

Living is
easier when the other is more important
than myself.

I experience many difficulties
when I take myself too
seriously.

Curiosity, the mantra,
non-resistance, the focus,
heartfulness, the response.

October 7 E. Meredith
96

52

Trust one hundred percent!

Seeing,
feeling
value everywhere,

value is soft,
allowing participation,
it transforms.

Where no contradiction lies . . .
healing occurs.

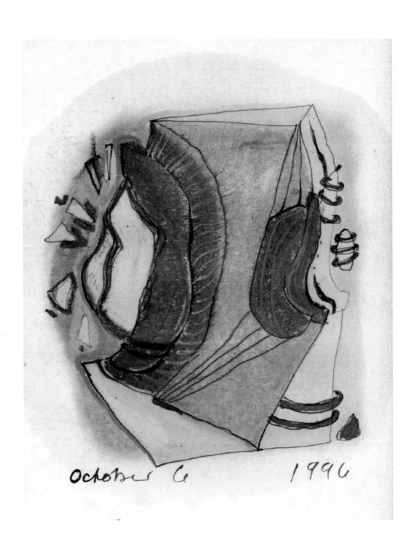

October 6   1996

Trust in source!

No need to manipulate,
if source requires me to
walk
on water . . .

I will!

There is absolutely no need to be anything
other
than I am!

The freedom to be here
without resisting to what's occurring,
in resonance,
ever aligning into
the symphony of stars
and roses,
crying and laughter of beingness,

I know
it is always you I find again,
in the eyes I love,
or in the misery I just felt . . .

Aaahh. . . .

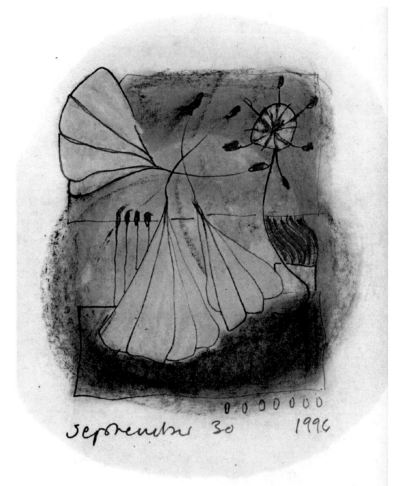

september 30   1996

The wind is rushing
over Jade Lake,
last leaves sailing,
scent of iris and violet root
rising.

My lips are parting
to feel the waters
curling around the earth.

Eyes open,
receiving forms into my
heart.

Opening windows,
breathing in the light.

Source's apprentice,
forever
tuning to the beloved within this
surprising field
of
miracles.

october 8   1990

Not usually perceived,
it is feeling,
and hearing too.

Sound-seeing color mixes...
sometimes shooting
like fireworks,
sound may rattle on the
back of my neck
or break right thru my whole body.

Colors can have the weirdest sounds,
they may vibrate,
soothingly,
or scream through the skin,
creating goosebumps on my bones.

Strange world.

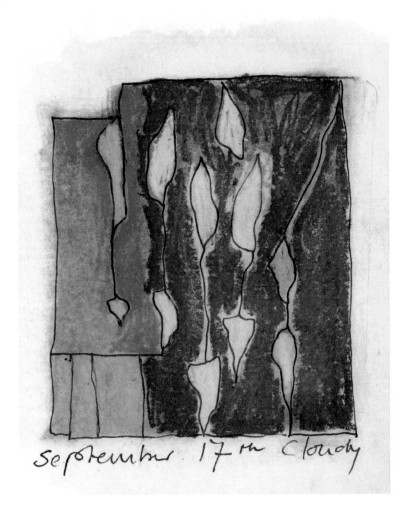

September 17th Cloudy

Sounds from somewhere
drum into my belly,
chimes touch my heart,
the top of my head tingles . . .

I ascend the ladder into the sky,
to find myself
in the guts of my being!

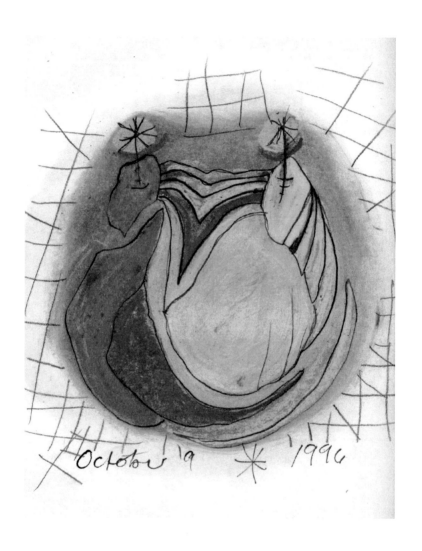

October 9 ✳ 1996

Spiral lights
coming
from the future,
dancing into the past,
peacock eyes
tremble
on the grass.

I receive to give,
give to receive . . .
breathing in,
breathing out.

Scents of summer,
lacy elderflowers,
white starclusters on earth,
secret teachings in plain sight,
impermanence,
my delight!

Inner connected,
independent,
back straight,
oh wonderous blueprint,
uniquely you,
exactly you!

Immortal beloved,
I can adore you in your
elegant summer dress of greens and gold,
colors and dots,
stripes and lines,
snakes, toads and cats appearing
on your makeup.

You are so numerous in
your presentation,
teasing me,
ever full of surprises,
just how I like it!

Our conditioning is to see
a slice of the picture
and then feel trapped
by it,
crying . . .
suffering.

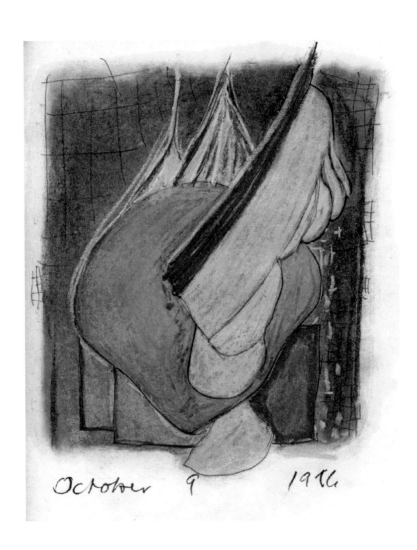

October 9   1916

Round and round
go the slaves
of my being . . .

I smile from within my
lover's embrace,

freeing them one by one.

october 1   1996

Your mind is looping!

Just open the next door,
just open it.

It is that easy.

We are the ones
we have been waiting for,
and now . . .
end of story?

Can we continue without
preconceived ideas,
fresh and heartful?

Heaven and earth
as one,
authentic,
no shame or guilt?

Shining,
sharing our gifts,
innate talents unique,
no need for competition . . .
trust,
hearts creating,
searching to enhance,
completing each other
in joyful expansion,
its up to you
and me.

The monsters in their
cupboard had their day.
We embrace them,
smile them into light
to brighten our day!

October 10   1996

Being older now . . .
truth-love . . .
however it comes,
soft or fierce.

There is not so much need to be loved,
because love already is . . .
not so much need
to be seen or heard.

As you become silvery,
you are the provider,
what you desire you give first.
You realize interdependence,
what you put out
is felt instantly,
whatever you perceive is experienced
right away.

You are there for what happens,
infinite good
with no opposites
comes in mysterious ways.
Joy expanding by
itself . . .
after breathing,
love is.

October 17   E. Meredith
76

This is the song I sing,
choose, choose and choose again.

It is up to you,
tune into your station of
passion and interest. . .
hum it up,

the sound of immortality
and elegance,
a new pattern
of sufficiency and creativity.

Outdated is separation...
baggage, a waste of energy,
love a direct harmonic congruency,
a hologram of fluid divinity,

non-local sparkle on my
nose, diamonds on your toes.

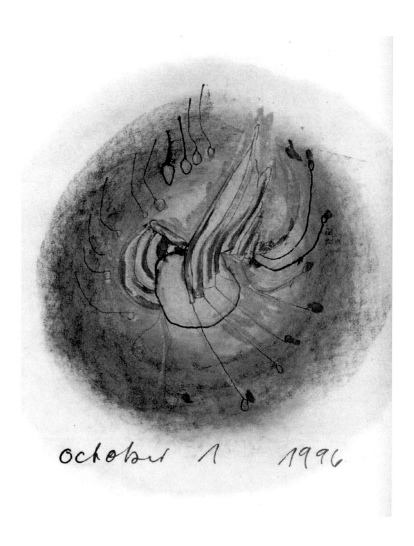

october 1   1996

An invitation . . .

sail with me, my beloved,
on this long journey
into the heart.

Just a little courage,
I hold your hand,
let go what no longer serves you.

Lay down your old beliefs
and soar into beingness.
Leave secrets behind
of "loving" and "not loving,"
a story in vain.

Part that curtain,
look through the window
and feel your heart.
The dreamer
is awakening!

The story looks like evolution,
spinning wheels,
a looping mind on
a merry-go-round.

Our mandala is a lightship,
a dimensional energy pattern
of clear light . . . waiting.

It arises out of the mire
of delusions
into unspeakable love
and clarity,
sailing into is-ness.

Freedom is nestled within the seeming limitations
of duality.

Open and read your earth book,
accept this body fully,
joy rises by itself.

Everything is close...
heaven and hell tempt you
to believe in
separation,
while the perfection
lies within you.
Forget the grasping,
melt back into my
embrace.
Feel this body,

your earth-space
vehicle.
You will find me there,
Loving you always,
Never separate.

As you sail the seas
Relax into the light
and listen to our sound, yours and mine.

Feel the texture of duality, touch and be touched,
it is all me smiling back at you.

In our hearts' wisdom
you are infinitely valuable,
beyond compare.

Let go of chains,
outdated habits
forming this world.

The "should's,
could's,
would's
and
trying to's"
are disappearing.

Courage,
feel . . .
allow the pain,
the pleasure,
expand your horizon,

free of judgment,
in innocence,
finding the heart's boundless joy.

Embrace the inevitable,
you can not go around it
or it will prolong the journey,
make harder the storms,
safe passage is
in non-resistance.

It is steep here,
non-negotiable,
accept what is happening,
take the challenge!

This is a bardo . . .
a transitional space,
where deities shout or whisper
sweetly,
just smile and relax,

trust the light.
I see your heart-
petals opening in the warmth
of the sun,
love unfolding.

Softly,
so simple and
intimate,
accept the union which you so crave . . .
soften again
and again.
Know there is nothing to
loose,
carried by your mandala,
the lightship that
I am.

Trust,
meet the challenge,
fears within or
stories without,
feel fully,
let the struggle go.

I smile,
take as much time as you need,
for love is ours.
Do not forget the roses,
for I am within them too,
holding hands.

I am in your cells, your blood,
the dewy grass,
trees ,
animals,
and all beings,
near and far, seen or not seen.
I am everywhere . . .
in kisses
and tears.

You are retuning
to essence,
joy unfolding,
no reason,
simply is.

With intent and passion
the dream disappears . . .

no more self-limiting
stories
of the looping mind.

In brilliant union . . .
joy propels
our diamondship
to adventures
beyond what is known.

I am
always home

liquid
self

home.

My structure is like
endless clouds
in wide open sky.

October 9 · ✳ · 1996

Peering into the cocoon,
I feel what is going on within.
The last of the caterpillar
just dissolved,
fully alive in to its essence,
fully alive!

No death, not one instant.
The fluid contains the butterfly
blueprint,
moving now,
like a baby
in its mother's belly.

New being forms,
burning the old away,
phoenix arising.

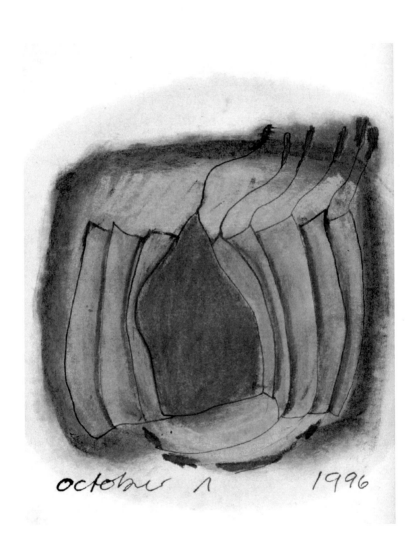

october 1   1996

I am
beyond fixing.

Good or bad,
love is,
shining always.

Even if it was momentarily dark
and I blinded myself
with fear.

Let the story go
and bask in love's ray
again.

ABOUT THE AUTHOR

Yemana , born and raised in Switzerland, has practiced meditation in various traditions and has lived for over 30 years in East Meredith, New York.

The drawings were done as a non conceptual meditation practise.